Letter Getters

ISBN 0-936110-20-1
Library of Congress Catalog Card Number:98-90339
Copyright 1998 by Greta Rasmussen
All rights reserved. Printed in the U.S.A.

Tin Man Press
P.O. Box 219
Stanwood, WA 98292

1-800-676-0459

Letter Getters

For Language Development and Thinking Fun

By Ted and Greta Rasmussen

Doing "Letter Getters" can be a little like eating popcorn! It's hard to stop once you get started. Part of the fun is the curious way the "set-up" sentence or paragraph brings on a very satisfying feeling of accomplishment when a conclusion is reached.

Here's how the book works: The letters you see at the bottom of each activity represent the first letters of words that finish the sentence. To be successful, students must use the letter clues in a way that is both grammatical and logical. Thus, the activities in "Letter Getters" foster language development and encourage deductive thinking.

Not only do "Letter Getters" activities motivate children to read and write, they also encourage them to develop a feeling for the way language is put together. Regarding language development, consider this activity:

It's not polite to cough without . . . c   y   m

Obviously, "covering your mouth," not "cover your mouth," is the correct response.

In addition to this kind of experience with the language, rigorous deductive thinking is also essential in solving the word puzzles. For example:

Look at the mosquito bites on my arm. I really got bitten at the picnic yesterday. Next time, I'll wear a shirt with . . . l   s

In this case, the activity presents a problem (getting mosquito bites) that leads to a deduction, or conclusion, (the need for a long-sleeved shirt).

There are several ways the activities can be implemented: They can be used as posters, at learning centers, as bulletin boards or on overheads for whole-class discussion. For your convenience, the pages are perforated and will tear out easily. The graphics are bold enough to be seen from a distance.

Regardless of how the activities are presented, one thing is for sure. You are missing a bet if you don't extend the activities by letting students make up their own "Letter Getters." The results might not be perfect, but youngsters will be thinking and writing!

Here are a few examples of "Letter Getters" written by students. They come from gifted and talented classes taught by Eileen Berkowitz in the Northeast Independent School District in San Antonio:

When I want to watch TV and my brother wants to watch something else, w a f (we always fight).

After breakfast my mom always tells me to g b y t (go brush your teeth).

The three most terrifying words to a lazy person are g a j (get a job).

The angry teacher looked at Michael and said, "Okay, young man, what is your excuse this time?" m d a m h (My dog ate my homework.)

* * * *

Extensions can also come from the subject matter itself. Since the topics focus on things children already know something about, ancillary activities are easy to invent. Here are examples for extending the first ten activities:

Activity 1: When people are happy, they smile. Think of three ways a dog expresses happiness. Think of three ways a cat expresses happiness.

Activity 2: Draw a picture of your favorite kind of pizza, showing all the ingredients.

Activity 3: Speaking of reaching, who's the tallest member in your family? The second tallest? What's the tallest animal you've ever seen?

Activity 4: Finish this thought: I remember the time when I lost my first tooth. It was . . .

Activity 5: Sunglasses can look very cool. Draw your face. Then draw yourself wearing cool sunglasses.

Activity 6: The word "hiccups" sounds like the sound it expresses. Make up another word for hiccups that is close to the way it sounds. It shouldn't be a real word.

Activity 7: On the subject of being scared . . . think of creepy, crawly insects. Which one scares you the most and why?

Activity 8: If you could choose to have 100 one-dollar bills or one $100 bill, and you wanted to keep from spending the money as long as possible, which would probably be the better choice? Explain your answer.

Activity 9: Draw a picture of your favorite ice-cream sundae or banana split and put a little sign beside every ingredient you used in "building" your dream dessert.

Activity 10: Think of two words that have the most to do with a beach. Write them.

* * * *

We have tried to put the easiest activities at the first of the book, and we suggest that you start with them. Of course, a "Letter Getter" that is easy for one child might be hard for another. When a student does get stuck on a particular problem, simply supply a strategic word and see if that helps.

We have presented the letter clues without punctuation or capitalization simply to keep the premise more pure. If you want students to include periods and question marks in their answers, we leave that . . .

u t y

In the meantime, we hope you enjoy this book and that your students become enthusiastic "Letter Getters!"

Greta and Ted Rasmussen

The Activities

I am taking your picture. Look straight at the camera. Now give me a . . .

b   s

If you have dough, tomato sauce, pepperoni, cheese, and some spices, you can . . .

m   a   p

Could you help me please? I need that box of cereal, but it's on the top shelf and I can't . . .

r   i

I can't leave it alone. I wiggle it with my tongue all the time. I . . .

h a l t

You shouldn't look directly at the sun because it might . . .

h   y   e

I always try to get rid of the hiccups the same way each time. I just . . .

h   m   b

My cat's back is arched and her fur is standing straight up. I think she . . .

j   s   a   d

If you could have 10 nickels or 5 quarters, which . . .

w   y   c

I like most kinds of ice cream, but my favorites are . . .

c   a   v

I am going to the beach with my aunt. She's supposed to pick me up in 10 minutes. I have lots of time to get ready, though, because my aunt is . . .

a   l

Birds use their wings to fly. Fish use their tails . . .

t s

It's hard to peel an orange, but it's easy to . . .

p a b

I'm glad pencils have erasers because sometimes I . . .

m   m

First, you play.
Then, I'll play.
Games are fun
when you . . .

† †

The ball hit me in the nose so hard, I was afraid . . .

i w b

When you cross a street, it is important to . . .

l   b   w

It's not polite to cough without . . .

c   y   m

Think about it. A comb has teeth, some chairs have arms, and tables . . .

h   l

Last month, my dog had five puppies. It's wonderful that a tiny puppy can grow . . .

i a b d

The hot cocoa looked delicious – all brown and marshmallowy, with steam coming up from the cup. Then I took a sip. Ouch! I . . .

b m t

The clouds are racing by.
The sky is very dark.
There is thunder in the
distance. You don't have
to be a genius to know
that soon . . .

i w r

I was in a piano recital and there were many people in the audience. I was scared that I wouldn't do well. I did okay, though, because when I finished . . .

e   c

I know I had a quarter but now I can't find it. I'll bet that it fell . . .

o   o   m   p

It's a fact. Plants will die if you forget to . . .

w   t

I played outside so long that now I am hot and thirsty. I need a . . .

d   o   w

It's hard to look up a word in the dictionary when you don't know how . . .

t   s   i

If you stand on one leg long enough, your . . .

l   w   g   t

I have a lucky number but I won't . . .

t   y   w   i   i

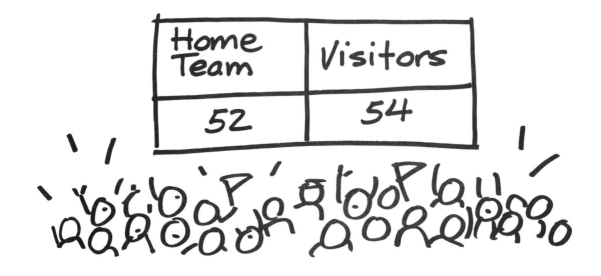

First, our team was ahead. Then, their team was ahead. Then, our team was ahead. Then, their team was ahead. We . . .

l t g

I eat several raisins at a time, but I eat grapes . . .

o   a   a   t

Look at the mosquito bites on my arms. I really got bitten at the picnic yesterday. Next time, I'll wear a shirt with . . .

l s

Our refrigerator has lots of magnets on it. I guess that's where magnets belong, because if you tried to put them on a wall, they would . . .

f   o

You could use a calculator to add 4 + 4, but it's just as easy to do it . . .

i   y   h

I can't give you an answer, because I didn't . . .

h t q

I am watching an ant crawl along the sidewalk. It isn't going very fast. I wonder where it came from and . . .

w　　i　　i　　g

Mary spent her birthday money on clothes. She bought a shirt, some pants, a dress, a necklace, and a sweater. Mary had a lot of . . .

m   t   s

One day, I was talking to my best friend on the phone. We talked and talked. Then my mother came home. She wasn't happy. She had tried calling me from work but . . .

t   l   w   b

I write with my right hand. I eat with my right hand. If you threw me a ball right now, I would . . .

c　　i　　w　　m　　r　　h

Sometimes, my dad makes homemade bread. I love to smell it baking in the oven. I love it so much that it makes . . .

m m w

Sneezing is funny. Do you think people all over the world say "achoo?"
Uh-oh. I feel a sneeze coming on right now.
Here it comes. Achoo! . . .

e   m

My dog is usually very calm. But lately, she's been scratching a lot. Last night I looked at her fur and . . .

f a f

I like to play checkers with my little sister, but she doesn't always like to play with me. Maybe the reason is that I . . .

a   w

Our family is planning a vacation trip next summer. My brother wants to go to Maine. My dad wants to go to Idaho. My mom wants to go to Texas. I like all those places, so I don't care . . .

w   w   g

We have a new student in our class. His name is Roberto. He comes from a city 100 miles from here. My desk is right next to his. I hope he likes me. I want . . .

t   b   h   f

Who dropped the ice-cream cone? It's all over the floor. Accidents happen, but whoever did it should . . .

c   i   u

Maria looked at herself in the mirror. Her new haircut was awful. Oh well, she thought, it . . .

w   g   b

My dad saw me throw a piece of popcorn up in the air and try to catch it in my mouth. He told me to stop doing that. He said that I. . .

m　　c

Have you ever listened to a joke and not understood it? When that happens to me, I laugh anyway. No one knows that I don't . . .

g   i

Susan has a very cool ring. One day, she let me try it on, but it was too . . .

l   f   m   f

When I walked into the place where the pigs were kept, it was so smelly that I had to . . .

h   m   n

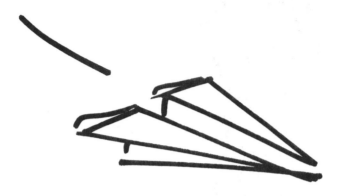

I need something to do. I have this piece of paper in front of me. I guess I will fold it into an airplane. Then I'll throw it and see how . . .

f i g

When I stand on my hands, my hair hangs down. My grandpa doesn't have that problem because he can't stand on his hands, and anyway . . .

h i b

Sometimes, I get very angry. But I have learned that before I say anything, it's a good idea to take a deep breath and . . .

c † †

If you always spell things backwards, you are not going to do well on a spelling test. But if the spelling words are "pop" and "noon" and "mom," you'll get a . . .

v   g   g

Little children learn how to scribble before they . . .

l   h   t   w

Walking around the mall is fun, even when you don't . . .

b   a

Every school night I have to go to bed at a certain time, but on the weekends, I . . .

g t s u l

Have you ever said the same word over and over until it doesn't even sound like the same word? Try saying "donkey" 20 times. Doesn't it . . .

s   s

If someone offered you a raw oyster, would you eat it or say . . .

n   t

Once I had a dream that I could fly. My arms grew feathers, and every time I flapped them, I . . .

† o

I could tell he wasn't really reading because the magazine was . . .

u d

Last night I slept on my arm a funny way. When I woke up, it really tingled! My . . .

a   w   a

Drawing horses is very hard to do. Drawing cats is easier. Drawing turtles is . . .

e   o   a

I know I'm in trouble when my mom tells me to . . .

g t m r

I'm having fun learning to draw. If you'll hold still for a while, I'll . . .

d　　y　　p

When I got home from school, my foot was really hurting. I had a blister on my heel. I guess that means I won't be wearing those . . .

n s t s t

How much do most people know about hyenas? Chances are . . .

n   m

The biggest difference between a city and a town is that a city . . .

h   m   p

Once you learn how to ride a bike . . .

y   n   f

When I was little, I used to think you grew taller only on your birthday. Now I . . .

k b

The trip was long and I was getting tired of riding in the car. I kept asking, How long until . . .

w　　　g　　　t

When I line up for lunch, I don't care where I am in line. If I'm first, that's fine. If I'm last, that's fine. But I don't like people who cut in rather than . . .

w † †

When you walk into your house at night, the first thing you do is . . .

t　　o　　t　　l

Stop it! I don't want ice down my back. If you do it again, I'm going to . . .

t o y

Sue told Debbie that she would keep what Debbie told her a secret. Then Sue turned around and told Debbie's secret to someone else, even though she had . . .

p   n   t   t

When Tom was at the store, he found a billfold. He picked it up, looked inside, and saw a lot of money. Then Tom gave the billfold - and the money - to the store manager. Tom . . .

d t r t

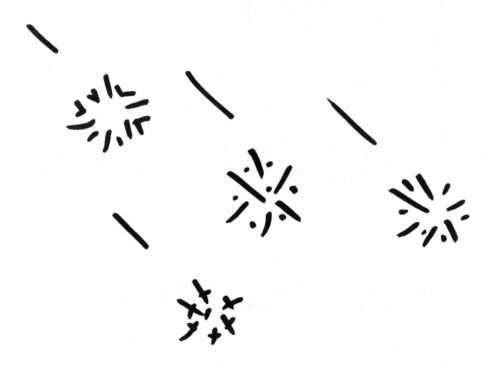

Every snowflake has a different shape. Every penny has . . .

t s s

Habits are hard to break. When I was little, I always looked under my bed before going to sleep. And you know what? I . . .

s   d

Halfway through telling the story, I realized I couldn't remember . . .

t   e

Sand is really just tiny . . .

p   o   r

I'm very pleased that I'm learning how to swim because I used to be . . .

s   o   t   w

I can tell what that present is because I can . . .

s   t   t   p

When a school bus has its red lights flashing, all . . .

c   m   s

Treating other people the way you would like to be treated is just a . . .

g   i

Yesterday was boring.
I didn't want to
watch TV or read
a book. My best friend
was gone. I just stayed
in my room feeling . . .

s   f   m

I tried to read the book but there were many words I didn't know. I kept having to go to the dictionary all the time. The book was . . .

t h f m

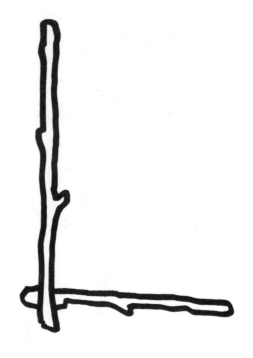

You can make the letter L by using two sticks. To make the letter W . . .

y   w   n   f   s

Sometimes when it rains, I put little sticks in puddles of water and . . .

p   t   a   b

You can't see stars in the daytime because the . . .

s i t b

Before I blew out the candles on my birthday cake, I closed . . .

m e a m a w

I love bubblegum, and blowing bubbles is fun – as long as you don't spend half your time peeling it . . .

o   y   f

My dog's name is Ralph. He knows his name and comes when I call him. My pet turtle's name is Cindy. She is cute, but she doesn't come when I call her by name. I guess that proves that . . .

d   a   s   t   t

It is hard to fly a kite when . . .

t w i n b

I like to eat cookies by taking lots of tiny little bites. When I do this, cookies always . . .

l a l t

It's hard to make snowballs with mittens on, so I took them off and used my bare hands. I couldn't make many, though, because . . .

m   h   g   t   c

I got to the parade late, and I couldn't see very well because there were so . . .

m p i f o m

I can read so well now that my little brother is always asking me to . . .

r   h   a   s

If I go to bed when I'm not tired, it sometimes takes me . . .

a   l   t   t   g   t   s

If you want to be a doctor, you have to . . .

g t s f a l t

You can't walk all the way around the world because there are . . .

o　　i　　t　　w

Answers

1. big smile.
2. make a pizza.
3. reach it.
4. have a loose tooth.
5. hurt your eyes.
6. hold my breath.
7. just saw a dog.
8. would you choose?
9. chocolate and vanilla.
10. always late.
11. to swim.
12. peel a banana.
13. make mistakes.
14. take turns.
15. it would bleed (it was broken).
16. look both ways.
17. covering your mouth.
18. have legs.
19. into a big dog.
20. burned my tongue.
21. it will rain.
22. everyone clapped.
23. out of my pocket.
24. water them.
25. drink of water.
26. to spell it.
27. leg will get tired.
28. tell you what it is.
29. lost the game.
30. one at a time.
31. long sleeves.
32. fall off.
33. in your head.
34. hear the question.
35. where it is going.
36. money to spend.
37. the line was busy.
38. catch it with my right hand.
39. my mouth water.
40. excuse me.
41. found a flea.
42. always win.
43. where we go.
44. to be his friend.
45. clean it up.
46. will grow back.
47. might choke.
48. get it.
49. large for my finger (little for my finger).
50. hold my nose.
51. far it goes (far it glides).
52. he is bald.
53. count to ten.
54. very good grade.

55. learn how to write.
56. buy anything.
57. get to stay up late.
58. sound strange (sound silly)?
59. no thanks.
60. took off.
61. upside down.
62. arm was asleep.
63. easiest of all.
64. go to my room.
65. draw your picture.
66. new shoes to school tomorrow.
67. not much.
68. has more people.
69. you never forget.
70. know better.
71. we get there?
72. waiting their turn.
73. turn on the light.
74. tell on you.
75. promised not to tell.
76. did the right thing.
77. the same shape.
78. still do.
79. the ending (the end).
80. pieces of rock.
81. scared of the water.
82. see through the paper.
83. cars must stop.
84. good idea.
85. sorry for myself.
86. too hard for me.
87. you would need four sticks.
88. pretend they are boats.
89. sun is too bright (sky is too bright).
90. my eyes and made a wish.
91. off your face.
92. dogs are smarter than turtles.
93. the wind is not blowing.
94. last a long time.
95. my hands got too cold.
96. many people in front of me.
97. read him a story.
98. a long time to get to sleep.
99. go to school for a long time.
100. oceans in the way.

Publications by Tin Man Press

Is It Friday Already? Learning Centers That Work – 30 weeks of centers in nine subject areas.

Are They Thinking? – A comprehensive, year-long thinking skills program.

Loosen Up! – Art activities designed to build confidence.

T is for Think – More than 300 drawings spur thinking excitement.

OPQ – Offbeat Adventures with the Alphabet – A center approach based on the alphabet.

Waiting for Lunch – Sponge activities for those little moments in the day.

Great Unbored Bulletin Board Books I and II – 20 great board ideas in each book.

Great Unbored Blackboard Book – Quick analytical activities you do on the board.

WakerUppers – 50 friendly hand-drawn reproducible sheets to motivate thinking.

Nifty Fifty – 500 provocative questions about 50 everyday things.

Smart Snips – Each of the 50 reproducible activities starts with something to cut.

Ideas To Go – 50 different assignments cover a broad range of thinking skills.

Brain Stations – 50 easy-to-make centers promote creative and flexible thinking.

Play by the Rules – 50 scripted challenges turn students into better listeners.

The Discover! Series – 24 card sets provide hands-on experiences with everyday objects.

Adventures of a Dot Series – 10 card sets use a Dot character to encourage thinking.

Linework – Jumbo card set centers around the concept of line.

An Alphabet You've Never Met – Jumbo card set plays creatively with letters.

Going Places – Students participate in five interesting imaginary adventures.

Letter Getters – Letter clues encourage language development and deductive thinking.

1-800-676-0459